The New US Security Agenda

Brian Fonseca • Jonathan D. Rosen

The New US Security Agenda

Trends and Emerging Threats

Brian Fonseca
Jack D. Gordon Institute for
   Public Policy
Florida International University
Miami, Florida, USA

Jonathan D. Rosen
Florida International University
Miami, Florida, USA

ISBN 978-3-319-84341-4   ISBN 978-3-319-50194-9   (eBook)
DOI 10.1007/978-3-319-50194-9

Cover image © John Burdumy, Moment / Getty Images
Cover design: Thomas Howey

Printed on acid-free paper

This Palgrave Macmillan imprint is published by Springer Nature
The registered company is Springer International Publishing AG
The registered company address is: Gewerbestrasse 11, 6330 Cham, Switzerland

ACKNOWLEDGMENTS

We would like to thank the editors and staff at Palgrave Macmillan for the opportunity to publish this book. It has been a pleasure working with the very talented and dedicated individuals who work at this publishing house.

Thanks to Florida International University (FIU) and FIU's Jack. D. Gordon Institute for Public Policy. The faculty and staff at the university and the institute have provided tremendous support to our academic endeavors while working at FIU.

A special thanks to Vanessa Rayan for her assistance copy-editing the manuscript. Thanks also to several anonymous peer reviewers who provided excellent suggestions that helped us improve the quality of the book. In addition, we would like to thank Fred Quintana for his helpful comments about potential policy recommendations.

Finally, Brian Fonseca would like to thank his wife, Maggie, and children, Derek and Kate, for their love and support throughout this process.

CONTENTS

1 Introduction   1

2 Countering Transnational Organized Crime   17

3 Immigration and Border Security   59

4 Cybersecurity in the US: Major Trends and Challenges   87

5 Countering Violent Extremism and Terrorism   107

6 Energy and Environmental Security   135

7 The Rise of External Actors: Paper Tigers
  or Security Threats?   161

8 Analytic Conclusions   183

Selected Bibliography   195

Index   199

LIST OF FIGURES

Fig. 2.1   Violent gang safe street task force arrests   42
Fig. 3.1   Number of deportations by homeland security (in thousands)   64
Fig. 3.2   Number of non-criminals deported by homeland security
           (in thousands)   64
Fig. 3.3   Number of people deported by homeland security (in thousands)   65
Fig. 5.1   Number of suicide terror attacks (2000–2008)   109
Fig. 5.2   Number of deaths from suicide terror attacks (2000–2008)   109
Fig. 5.3   Number of suicide terror attacks (2009–2015)   110
Fig. 5.4   Deaths from suicide terror attacks (2009–2015)   110
Fig. 5.5   Number of suicide terrorist attacks   118
Fig. 7.1   Global defense spending in 2014 in millions   166

LIST OF TABLES

Table 4.1   Number of cybersecurity incidents reported by US Federal
            Agencies (FY 2006–2014)   95
Table 4.2   President Obama's FY 2016 budget proposal   96

CHAPTER 1

Introduction

On November 16, 2016, members of the Islamic State of Iraq and Syria (ISIS), a terrorist organization, attacked several venues in Paris, France, including a concert, cafes, bars, and soccer match, killing 129 people and injuring another 350 people. The French government mobilized its resources and security apparatuses searching for Abdelhamid Abaaoud, the alleged leader of the attack. François Hollande, the president of France, declared: "Our democracy has prevailed over much more formidable opponents than these cowardly assassins."[1] He vowed to retaliate and find the individuals responsible for such atrocious attacks. On December 2, 2015, a husband and wife team, Tashfeen Malik and Syed Rizwan Farook, launched an attack against the Indland Regional Center in San Bernardino, California. The shooting rampage resulted in 22 people injured and the deaths of 14 others, sparking outrage among the US and panic among many individuals.[2] Questions began to arise in the US about the linkages between the couple and ISIS. It was noted that "Malik made a public declaration of loyalty to ISIS' leader while the attack was underway."[3] What ensued in the US was intense debates about Islamic extremism and immigration policies since the wife came to the US on a fiancé visa.

The 2016 US presidential candidates responded quickly to the attacks and raised major questions about immigration policies as a result of the events in Paris. Republican frontrunner and the eventual nominee for the presidency, Donald Trump, sent shockwaves across the US and the world when he called for the banning of all Muslims traveling to the US. He argued that the US should have a "total and complete shutdown of

© The Author(s) 2017
B. Fonseca, J.D. Rosen, *The New US Security Agenda*,
DOI 10.1007/978-3-319-50194-9_1

1

Muslims entering the United States until our country's representatives can figure out what is going on."[4] Trump harped on the fact that the US needs to be able to control and screen the people coming into the country to prevent further attacks from occurring. He contended that the ban could be temporary, but the US government needs a better way to keep track of who is entering the country. He stated, "Until we are able to determine and understand this problem and the dangerous threat it poses, our country cannot be the victims of horrendous attacks by people that believe only in Jihad, and have no sense of reason or respect for human life."[5] Trump's comments angered many people as critics called him a racist promoting intolerance. Islam is the fastest growing religion in the world, and the number of Muslims is expected to increase drastically in the coming years. In 2010, for example, 1.6 billion Muslims existed in the world, but this number will proliferate by 73 percent in 2050 to 2.8 billion. Michael Lipka and Conrad Hackett stated that "[b]y 2050, Muslims will be nearly as numerous as Christians, who are projected to remain the world's largest religious group at 31.4% of the global population."[6] Trump was criticized by not only the Democrats but also fellow Republicans. Former Vice President Dick Cheney argued that Trump's policy "goes against everything we stand for and believe in."[7] Across the pond, in the UK, a petition began to circulate in December 2015 that called for the banning of Trump from entering the UK. A spokesman from Downing Street remarked that David Cameron, the prime minister of the country, was highly critical of Trump's malicious comments, asserting that his remarks were "divisive, unhelpful and quite simply wrong."[8]

The aforementioned events highlight one of the major issues on the national security agenda of the US: the emergence of radical violent extremism. The rise of radical extremism and combating terrorism is on the minds of many Americans—as well as others around the world. Intense debates have occurred about how to combat extremist groups, such as the rise of ISIS in Syria.

Violent extremism, however, is not the only security issue on the agenda of countries, particularly the US. Topics, such as global warming, have become very important on the national security agenda. The increases in global temperatures have caused the sea level to rise: global sea levels spiked by 6.7 inches over the past 100 years, and the rates have continued to accelerate. For instance, the rate of global sea level rise has almost doubled over the last century, demonstrating that the problem has continued to worsen and presents major threats in terms of the plethora of environmental impacts.[9] Divya Srikanth argues that "[c]limate change has assumed critical importance to world security in the last few decades. Global warming due to climate change has been predicted to have a cascading affect, wherein the increasing temperatures will facilitate more frequent formation of cyclones and storms in the tropical regions and the melting of polar ice caps, in turn leading to rising sea levels and possible submerging of low-lying areas and island nations, threatening their very existence."[10] In the future, many cities will be destroyed as a result of sea level rise. Research indicates that 14 US cities will not exist in the next 100 years as a result of the consequences of global warming, including: Savannah, Seattle, Virginia Beach, Charleston, Los Angeles, San Diego, Sacramento, New Orleans, Honolulu, Atlantic City, New York City, Boston, Fort Lauderdale, and Miami.[11]

In addition to global warming, energy security remains a major issue on the security agenda of the twenty-first century. Countries will continue to search for energy sources in order to meet their energy demands. The US imported 11 million barrels of oil per day in 2008, demonstrating its high level of dependence on other countries for this key resource. By 2025, it is predicted that the US will decrease the number of barrels of oil imported each day by 33 percent, which is a large improvement from the current levels.[12] New techniques that have been highly controversial, such as hydraulic fracturing, or "fracking," are being utilized and are hotly debated among experts.[13]

Along with energy security, another major issue on the national security agenda of the US—and other countries—that will continue to increase in importance every day is cybersecurity.[14] Riley Walters argues that "[c]oncerns continue to grow as both the number of attacks on companies' networks and the cost to companies are increasing. The quantity and quality of information being hacked, stolen, destroyed, or leaked is becoming more of a problem for consumers and businesses alike."[15] Cyber-attacks continue to increase and represent a major national security challenge as attackers can not only shutdown grid systems and steal information but also impact the global economy. Cyberterrorists and hackers must only be successful one time to have severe impacts, while companies and governments must constantly prevent against attacks. Art Gilliland, the Hewlett-Packard enterprise security vice president, reiterates this point, arguing: "Adversaries only need to be successful once to gain access to your data, while their targets must be successful every time to stop the barrage of attacks their organizations face each day."[16] This issue will likely only continue to worsen.

The goal of this book is to understand the security challenges that exist in the twenty-first century, from climate change to drug trafficking and organized crime. While the topics, such as transnational organized crime (TOC), are global in nature, the book focuses on US national security and the new security agenda of the twenty-first century.[17] This work seeks to answer the following questions: What are the major security challenges that exist in the twenty-first century? How have the threats evolved and how can such threats best be addressed? How can scholars and policy analyst understand the new security agenda in conceptual terms? The book concludes with several policy proposals in order to bridge the divide between academia and the policy world.

THEORETICAL APPROACHES TO SECURITY STUDIES

Security concerns have always been a major concern of International Relations (IR) scholars. Realism has dominated the IR literature for decades and much of the research evolved under the context of the Cold War, where the two superpowers, the US and the Soviet Union, battled for control of the international system. In his groundbreaking 1959 work, *Man, the State, and War: A Theoretical Analysis*,[18] Kenneth Waltz argued that there are three levels of analysis for understanding and studying international relations. The first level has to do with human nature arguments and the role of the individual for explaining why wars and conflict occur. The second level, the state, deals with the internal dynamics of the state and how these factors can contribute to conflict. Finally, the third level is the international system. Realism is broken down into various camps from classical to offensive and defensive realists. Classical realists, like E.H. Carr and Hans Morgenthau,[19] focus on the role of human nature and apply such characteristics to states. Tim Dunne and Brian C. Schmidt explain the relationship between human nature and the state, arguing that "[t]he behaviour of the state as a self-seeking egoist is understood to be merely a reflection of the characteristics of the people that comprise the state. It is human nature that explains why international politics is necessarily power politics."[20] States, therefore, have two positions in the international system: they can dominate or be dominated.

Kenneth Waltz published *Theory of International Politics* in 1979, arguing that the third level of analysis, the international system, is the defining feature for understanding international relations. Waltz focuses on the structure of the international system, which is anarchical in nature.[21]

Anarchy, however, does not refer to chaos but rather the fact that there is no overarching government or global government that can come to the rescue of states if there is a problem. John Mearsheimer refers to this as the 9-1-1 problem as the states cannot call for help in the event of an emergency as there is no global government or world police to come to the rescue. The number one goal of states is to survive in this self-help world.[22]

Much of the IR literature during the Cold War focused on nuclear proliferation and state security, which is quite logical given events such as the Cuban Missile Crisis in 1962 and the concern that the US and the Soviet Union,[23] both of which had nuclear weapons, could strike and lead to a nuclear war. One of the most important concepts developed in IR is the notion of Mutually Assured Destruction (MAD).[24] The logic is that two countries with nuclear weapons could lead to a nuclear race as one country increases the number of nuclear weapons that it has. In other words, if country A decides to increase its nuclear stockpile, country B will increase its nuclear capacity because it feels less secure. Therefore, two countries that have nuclear weapons are safer as both countries will be deterred from striking since the two states both have the capacity to destroy one another. Ultimately, MAD leads to deterrence.

Structural realists focus on the structure of the international system and the balance of power. Two key divides exists between neo-realists: offensive and defensive realists. Neo-realists argue that states are black boxes or billiard balls. As in the game of billiards, the countries, like billiard balls, crash into each other, which is similar to the international system where states inevitably conflict over issues of power and dominance in the international system.[25] States are considered black boxes because all states regardless of the internal dynamics, political system, economic system, and other internal factors have the same goal: survive. Countries that have the capacity seek to increase their capabilities in order to become hegemons. A difference exists between offensive and defensive realists with regard to the desired level of power. Offensive realists believe that state should always seek to maximize power and become the regional hegemon. John Mearsheimer, an offensive realist, argues that a state that has the capacity should never be satisfied with its level of military power and constantly seek to strengthen in power to avoid other potential conflicts. He asserts that it is not possible for a country to be a global hegemon due to two factors: the sea and geography. According to Mearsheimer, great powers should seek to be the hegemon of their geographic regions.[26]

Realists, however, disagree with regard to the optimal level of power desired by states. Defensive realists believe that too much power can cause the balance of power to shift as other states will balance against a country if they view it as a threat or too powerful.[27] Therefore, a state with the capability should attempt to become the hegemon but should not seek to constantly increase power, as described by offensive realists,[28] since such behavior could have negative repercussions. In other words, the hegemon should focus on maintaining the status quo.

Various criticisms have emerged with regard to realism. First, realists are concerned with great powers in the international system. The logic is that in order to understand international relations scholars must focus on the most powerful states in the international system. Of the approximately 200 countries in the world, only a handful of countries have the military and economic capability to project force. Realists view weaker powers as irrelevant to understanding the international system as they can simply align with other countries in order to balance against other powers.[29] Realists focus on great powers and seek to answer questions related to the international system, power politics, and nuclear proliferation, among other issues, ignoring many other important issues that other countries around the globe face.[30]

For realists, security is about state security. Realists have limitations as they are focused on traditional security threats such as wars and nuclear attacks.[31] Since the unit of analysis is the state, realists do not concentrate on other non-state actors, such as drug traffickers or terrorists. Divya Srikanth echoes such concerns and stresses the change in the security agenda away from non-state actors, declaring:

> The emergence of a number of non-state actors, such as terrorist networks, drug cartels and maritime piracy networks, and intra-state conflicts (e.g. civil wars) have assumed importance as new-age threats to the national security of present-day states. Apart from such non-state and transnational actors, the impact of environmental degradation on the future of the nation-state, especially the implications of global climate change, has emerged as a credible and serious threat to the future existence of modern-day nation-states.[32]

Realists fail to understand the complexity of the various security threats that exist as they focus on "high politics" and traditional security threats as opposed to non-traditional security threats (i.e. environmental and energy security). High politics are issues that are fundamental to the survival of a state, which is different than "low politics"—issues that are less vital to the national security and survival of a country. Michael Barnett argues:

> Power politics approaches to security policy focus on how the state's pursuit of military power and war-fighting potential is shaped by systemic forces. This gives explanatory primacy to the state's interaction with other

self-interested actors in the international system. Consequently, the implicit assumption is that "high politics," a state's security relationship with other states in the international system, is autonomous and therefore distinct from "low politics," societal pressures, and the domestic political economy. These studies almost uniformly assume that the domestic political economy and national security issues are separate and distinct spheres.[33]

The security agenda has evolved and many new issues such as climate change, economic security, and a plethora of other topics are crucial security issues that must be addressed. Donald C. Winter explains how the security agenda of the twenty-first century has evolved beyond the traditional security threats that plagued the US during the days of the Cold War, contending: "The national security situation in the 21st century is far different from what existed during the Cold War. Today, the U.S. faces a disturbingly diverse set of national security challenges ranging from pirates threatening U.S. citizens and world commerce off the coast of Somalia to transnational terrorist organizations, such as al-Qaeda, to rogue nations acquiring nuclear capabilities, such as North Korea."[34] In sum, realism is not sufficient for understanding the complex nature of the security challenges that exist today as realists focus on state security and high politics. Realists, therefore, fail to account for the nuances of the major security issues.

In 1983, Richard Ullman published an article titled "Redefining Security," arguing that the theoretical concept of security had to be expanded as so much of the literature focused on hard power: military security. Ullman argues that "[s]ince the onset of the Cold War in the late 1940s, every administration in Washington has defined American national security in excessively narrow and excessively military terms. Politicians have found it easier to focus the attention of an inattentive public on military dangers, real or imagined, than on nonmilitary ones."[35] Ullman highlights the inherent trade-offs that exist. For example, measures to increase security can lead to less civil liberties, with one example being the role of the National Security Agency (NSA) and the emergence of groups that have argued that the US government is infringing on the civil liberties of Americans. Ullman has also stressed the need to redefine the threats, stating: "In addition to examining security tradeoffs, it is necessary to recognize that security may be defined not merely as a goal but as a consequence-this means that we may not realize what it is or how important it is until we are threatened with losing it. In some sense, therefore, security is defined and valorized by the threats which challenge it."[36] Overall, Ullman's article is a watershed piece as the security studies literature during this period focused on hard power and state security and failed to understand the evolving nature of security. The challenge with the Ullman argument is that if everything is security, then nothing is security.[37]

Barry Buzan, Ole Wæver, and Jaap de Wilde published *Security: A New Framework for Analysis* in 1998.[38] In this work, the authors, who are referred to as the Copenhagen School, significantly advanced the security studies literature. Buzan, Wæver, and de Wilde are constructivists and argue that defining security depends on one's social construction or perception. The question becomes: security for whom and for what?[39] Buzan and his colleagues posit that there are levels and sectors that can be analyzed. In terms of sectors, there is the military, economic, environmental, political, and societal. The levels of analysis include the individual, society, national, and international.

Buzan, Wæver, and de Wilde highlight how the security agenda can change over time, focusing on how an issue can become elevated on the agenda (i.e. securitized). In order to understand how an issue becomes more important on the security agenda, it is important to analyze the discourse of leaders[40] to trace how the security agenda can change and evolve. The first issue is defining what constitutes a security problem? In other words, a security issue for one person might not be one for another individual. Buzan, Wæver, and de Wilde[41] focus on the conceptual terms of security, stating: "'Security' is the move that takes politics beyond the established rules of the game and frames the issue either as a special kind of politics or as above politics. Securitization can thus be seen as a more extreme version of politicization."[42] Discourse analysis enables scholars to examine if the security agenda has changed over time. The analysis of discourse (i.e. speech acts) alone, however, is insufficient as an actor can seek to securitize an issue but that does not necessarily mean this process was successful. Therefore, it is important to "follow the money" and analyze budgets.[43] If an issue was successfully securitized, then the resources will have been allocated to support the topic being elevated on the security agenda, or securitized.

An example would be the George W. Bush administration's launching of the global war on terror (GWOT) after the terrorist attacks on September 11, 2001. Bush made the fight against terrorism as the number one national security issue in the US despite the fact that many experts criticized the concept of a GWOT.[44] On September 21, 2001, George Bush spoke in front of a joint session of the US Congress, declaring: "Our war on terror begins with al Qaeda, but it does not end there. It will not end until every terrorist group of global reach has been found, stopped and defeated. Americans are asking, why do they hate us? They hate what we see right here in this chamber—a democratically elected government."[45] Bush stressed that the US government would invest its resources and do whatever it takes to win the war against terror. He stated, "Americans are asking: How will we fight and win this war? We will direct every resource at our command—every means of diplomacy, every tool of intelligence, every instrument of law enforcement, every financial influence, and every necessary weapon of war—to the disruption and to the defeat of the global terror network."[46] Bush's statements, however, were not merely rhetoric as he successfully securitized the war on terror as demonstrated by the proliferation in resources that the US government spent on fighting wars in Afghanistan and Iraq. Jesse Rifkin argues, "As of September 2014, total U.S. expenditures on the war in Iraq totaled $815.8 billion, about 93 percent of which was spent after 2003. That cost is more than 16 times the Bush administration's original projection."[47] As of March 2013, the estimated cost of the Iraq War, including payments to veterans, is over $2 trillion, demonstrating that the Bush administration successfully securitized the war.[48] Others, such as economist Joseph Stiglitz, argue that the total costs of the Iraq War have been more than $3 trillion.[49]

While the Copenhagen School emphasizes how an issue is securitized, these scholars focus less on how an issue moves from being on the security agenda to less of a priority—that is, how an issue is de-securitized.[50] Various works have elaborated on this issue, discussing how an issue moves from being a key security priority to less of a priority as well as how one defines success.[51] Determining whether the goals have been achieved depends on the definition of success and the perceptions of the people analyzing the issue.

Overall, the Copenhagen School is a major advancement in security studies because it moves beyond the traditional concepts of state security that the realists emphasize and focuses on other sectors and level of security analysis. The conceptual framework used by these scholars is also very clearly defined as the key sectors and levels are identified. This is a major concern in the Ullman article, which opened up the security agenda but the problem is that if everything is a security issue than nothing is a security issue. In sum, there are priorities on the security agenda and not every topic is given equal weight.

The evolution of security studies has also seen discussions about human security.[52] Many of the major security issues today, immigration, drug trafficking, organized crime, and climate change impact individuals.

It, therefore, is not possible to talk about security issues without examining the role of humans and human security. According to the Commission on Human Security, "Human security means protecting fundamental freedoms—freedoms that are the essence of life. It means protecting people from critical (severe) and pervasive (widespread) threats and situations. It means using processes that build on people's strengths and aspirations. It means creating political, social, environmental, economic, military and cultural systems that together give people the building blocks of survival, livelihood and dignity."[53] Thus, the key element of human security is how to protect individuals. According to P.H. Liotta and Taylor Owen, "At its core, human security is about protecting people. Despite the multiple, contending views that have emerged regarding human security since it gained prominence in the 1990s—ranging from viewing human security as a radical departure from 'traditional' security forms, to a focus on moderate evolutionary changes to the existing security infrastructure and mandate—the central feature of most arguments addresses how best to both protect and empower people."[54] Human security combines various "human elements" and is characterized by the following aspects: prevention-oriented, context-specific, people-centered, and comprehensive in nature.[55]

METHODOLOGICAL APPROACH

This work will apply a constructivist theoretical approach akin to the one used by Buzan and his colleagues at the Copenhagen School. In reality, constructivism is both a theoretical approach as well as a methodology. Buzan, Wæver, and de Wilde provide a methodological approach for studying security studies as they propose several methods for understanding the securitization process. This work will analyze discourse, or speech acts, made by authoritative figures regarding various issues in order to understand efforts to securitize several perceived threats. The challenge is to identify the key actors and analyze what they have said in an effort to examine which issues have become more important on the national security agenda of the US. Discourse alone, however, is insufficient as speaking about an issue does not mean that it has been successfully securitized. Along with focusing on discourse, this book will concentrate on financial resources to understand which issues have been more of a security priority on the agenda. This is best determined by analyzing which issue areas receive more resources. The Obama administration, for instance, has attempted to securitize some issues, such as environmental security, while it has sought to de-securitize/de-emphasize other issues, such as the war on terror. In terms of the time period, this book focuses on critical junctures in the twenty-first century that have impacted the security agenda of the US. National security doctrines evolve over time and this work is an effort to analyze the evolution of the security agenda, highlighting some of the new threats as well as some of the emerging threats.

VOLUME OVERVIEW

The next chapter focuses on countering TOC, highlighting the major security challenges as well as US policy. Chapter 3 addresses the issue of immigration and border security, which is a very important issue that is hotly debated. This chapter is followed by a chapter on cybersecurity. Chapter 5 examines violent extremism and terrorism and highlights the challenges and obstacles as well as US policies with regard to these issues during the Bush and Obama administrations. Chapter 6 explores two issues that are intricately related: environmental and energy security in the US. Chapter 7 analyzes the rise of external actors and examines whether this constitutes a major security threat for the US. This chapter is followed by the analytic conclusions, which provide policy recommendations.

NOTES

1. François Hollande quoted in Aurelien Breeden, Kimiko de Freytas-Tamura, Katrin Bennhold, "Call to Arms in France amid Hunt for Belgian Suspect in Paris Attacks," *The New York Times*, November 16, 2015.
2. "San Bernardino shooting updates," *Los Angeles Times*, December 9, 2015.
3. Faith Karimi, Jason Hanna, and Yousuf Basil, "San Bernardino shooters 'supporters' of ISIS, terror group says," *CNN*, December 5, 2015.
4. Donald Trump quoted in Russell Berman, "Donald Trump's Call to Ban Muslim Immigrants," *The Atlantic*, December 7, 2015.
5. Donald Trump quoted in Russell Berman, "Donald Trump's Call to Ban Muslim Immigrants."
6. Michael Lipka and Conrad Hackett, "Why Muslims are the world's fastest-growing religious group," *Pew Research Center*, April 23, 2015. http://www.pewresearch.org/fact-tank/2015/04/23/why-muslims-are-the-worlds-fastest-growing-religious-group/, accessed December 2015, p. 2.
7. Dick Cheney quoted in "Donald Trump's Muslim US ban call roundly condemned," *BBC News*, December 8, 2015.

8. David Cameron quoted in Nicholas Winning, "U.K. Petition Calls for Banning Donald Trump," *The Wall Street Journal*, December 9, 2015.
9. "Climate change: How do we know?" *Global Climate Change*, http://climate.nasa.gov/evidence/, December 2015.
10. Divya Srikanth, "Non-traditional Security Threats in the 21st Century: A Review," *International Journal of Development and Conflict*, 4 (2014): 60–68, especially p. 64.
11. "14 U.S. Cities That Could Disappear Over The Next Century, Thanks To Global Warming," *The Huffington Post*, August 26, 2013.
12. "FACT SHEET: America's Energy Security," *The White House*, March 30, 2011, https://www.whitehouse.gov/the-press-office/2011/03/30/fact-sheet-americas-energy-security, accessed December 2015.
13. *Fracking: The Promise And the Peril* (New York, N.Y.: The New York Times Company, 2015).
14. Peter W. Singer and Allan Friedman, *Cybersecurity and Cyberwar: What Everyone Needs to Know®* (New York, N.Y.: Oxford University Press, 2014).
15. Riley Walters, "Cyber Attacks on U.S. Companies Since November 2014," *The Heritage Foundation*, November 18, 2015, http://www.heritage.org/research/reports/2015/11/cyber-attacks-on-us-companies-since-november-2014, accessed December 2015, p. 1.
16. Art Gilliland quoted in AFP, "Cost of Cyber Attacks Jumps for US Firms: Study," *Security Week*, October 16, 2014.
17. For more on National Security, see: Donald M. Snow, *National Security for a New Era* (New York, N.Y.: Routledge, 2014); Ronald R. Krebs, *Narrative and the Making of US National Security* (Cambridge, U.K.: Cambridge University Press, 2015).
18. Kenneth N. Waltz, *Man, the State, and War: A Theoretical Analysis* (New York, N.Y.: Columbia University Press, 2001, first published in 1959).
19. Hans J. Morgenthau, *Politics Among Nations: The Struggle for Power and Peace* (New York, N.Y.: McGraw-Hill, 1993, first printed in 1948; this is the revised edition by Kenneth W. Thimpson); E.H. Carr, *The Twenty Years' Crisis: 1919–1939* (New York, N.Y.: Palgrave Macmillan, 2001, editor Michael Cox).
20. Tim Dunne and Brian C. Schmidt, "Realism," *The Globalization of World Politics: An Introduction to International Relations*, John Baylis, Steve Smith, and Patricia Owens, eds. (New York, N.Y.: Oxford University Press, 2011, fifth edition), p. 89.
21. Kenneth N. Waltz, *Theory of International Politics* (New York, N.Y.: McGraw-Hill, Inc, 2010, first edition 1979).
22. John J. Mearsheimer, *The Tragedy of Great Power Politics* (New York, N.Y.: W.W. Norton & Company, Inc., 2001).
23. Robert Jervis, *The Meaning of the Nuclear Revolution: Statecraft and the Prospect of Armageddon* (Ithaca, N.Y.: Cornell University Press, 1989).

24. Scott Douglas Sagan and Kenneth N. Waltz, *The Spread of Nuclear Weapons: An Enduring Debate* (New York, N.Y.: W. W. Norton & Company, 2012, third edition).
25. John J. Mearsheimer, *The Tragedy of Great Power Politics*.
26. John J. Mearsheimer, *The Tragedy of Great Power Politics*; John J. Mearsheimer, "A realist reply," *International Security* Vol. 20 No. 1 (1995): pp. 82–93; John J. Mearsheimer, "Structural realism," *International relations theories: Discipline and diversity* Vol. 83 (2007): pp. 83.
27. Robert Jervis, "Realism, neoliberalism, and cooperation: understanding the debate," *International Security* Vol. 24 No. 1 (1999): pp. 42–63; Robert Jervis, "Realism, game theory, and cooperation," *World Politics* Vol. 40 No. 03 (1988): pp. 317–349.
28. John J. Mearsheimer, *The Tragedy of Great Power Politics*; for more, see Glenn H. Snyder, "Mearsheimer's World—Offensive Realism and the Struggle for Security: A Review Essay," *International Security* Vol. 27 No. 1 (2002): pp. 149–173; Christopher Layne, "The 'Poster Child for offensive realism': America as a global hegemon," *Security Studies* Vol. 12 No. 2 (2002): pp. 120–164.
29. For an interesting discussion on the role of weak states in the international system, see: Hanna Samir Kassab, *Weak States in International Relations Theory: The Cases of Armenia, St. Kitts and Nevis, Lebanon, and Cambodia* (New York, N.Y.: Palgrave Macmillan, 2015).
30. Tim Dunne and Brian C. Schmidt, "Realism."
31. Bruce M. Bagley and Juan G. Tokatlian, "Dope and Dogma: Explaining the Failure of US-Latin America Relations in the 1990s," in *The United States and Latin America in the 1990s*, eds. Jonathan Hartlyn and Lars Schoultz (Chapel Hill: University of North Carolina, 1992), pp. 214–234.
32. Divya Srikanth, "Non-traditional Security Threats in the 21st Century: A Review," p. 60.
33. Michael Barnett, "High Politics is Low Politics: The Domestic and Systemic Sources of Israeli Security Policy, 1967–1977," *World Politics*, Vol 42, No. 4 (July 1990): pp. 529–562, especially p. 531.
34. The Honorable Donald C. Winter, "Adapting to the Threat Dynamics of the 21st Century," *The Heritage Foundation*, September 15, 2011. http://www.heritage.org/research/reports/2011/09/adapting-to-the-threat-dynamics-of-the-21st-century, accessed December 2015, p. 1.
35. Richard H. Ullman, "Redefining Security," *International Security*, Vol. 8, No. 1 (Summer 1983): pp 129–153, especially p. 129.
36. Richard H. Ullman, "Redefining Security," p. 133.
37. For more on security studies, see: Bruce M. Bagley, Jonathan D. Rosen, and Hanna S. Kassab, eds., *Reconceptualizing Security in the Americas in the Twenty-First Century* (Lanham, Maryland: Lexington Books, February 2015).

38. Barry Buzan, Ole Wæver, and Jaap de Wilde, *Security: A New Framework for Analysis* (Boulder, CO: Lynne Rienner, 1998).
39. Barry Buzan, Ole Wæver, and Jaap de Wilde, *Security: A New Framework for Analysis.*
40. This is referred to by these scholars as speech acts of authoritative figures.
41. Barry Buzan, Ole Wæver, and Jaap de Wilde, *Security: A New Framework for Analysis.*
42. Richard H. Ullman, "Redefining Security," p. 24.
43. See: Jonathan D. Rosen, *The Losing War: Plan Colombia and Beyond* (Albany, N.Y.: State University of New York, 2014).
44. Ivo H. Daadler and James M. Lindsay, *American Unbound: The Bush Revolution in Foreign Policy* (Hoboken, New Jersey: John Wiley & Sons, Inc., 2003; 2005); Bob Woodward, *Bush at War* (New York, N.Y.: Simon & Schuster, 2002); for more on the Bush administration and the war on terror, see: Susan Moeller, "Think Again: Bush's War on Terror," *Center for American Progress*, March 18, 2004, https://www.americanprogress.org/issues/security/news/2004/03/18/615/think-again-bushs-war-on-terror/, accessed January 2016.
45. "Text of George Bush's speech," *The Guardian*, September 21, 2000, p. 3.
46. "Text of George Bush's speech," p. 2.
47. Jesse Rifkin "'Mission Accomplished' Was 12 Years Ago Today. What's Been The Cost Since Then?" *The Huffington Post*, May 1, 2015, p. 1.
48. Daniel Trotta, "Iraq war costs U.S. more than $2 trillion: study," *Reuters*, March, 14, 2013.
49. Joseph E. Stiglitz and Linda J. Bilmes, *The Three Trillion Dollar War: The True Cost of the Iraq Conflict* (New York, N.Y.: W.W. Norton & Company, 2008).
50. For more, see Jonathan D. Rosen, *The Losing War: Plan Colombia and Beyond.*
51. Bruce M. Bagley, Jonathan D. Rosen, and Hanna S. Kassab, eds., *Reconceptualizing Security in the Americas in the Twenty-First Century.*
52. For more on alternative approaches to security studies and human security, see: J. Ann Tickner, "Continuing the conversation," *International Studies Quarterly* 42, no. 1 (1998): pp. 205–210; Roland Paris, "Human security: Paradigm shift or hot air?" *International security* 26, no. 2 (2001): pp. 87–102.
53. Quoted in United Nations, *Human Security in Theory and Practice: An Overview of the Human Security Concept and the United Nations Trust Fund for Human Security* (New York, N.Y.: UN, 2009), http://www.un.org/humansecurity/sites/www.un.org.humansecurity/files/human_security_in_theory_and_practice_english.pdf, accessed July 2016, p. 5; Commission on Human Security, *Human Security Now* (New York, N.Y.: Commission on Human Security, 2003), http://reliefweb.int/sites/reliefweb.int/files/resources/91BAEEDBA50C6907C1256D19006A9353-chs-security-may03.pdf, accessed July 2016.

54. Peter H Liotta and Taylor Owen, "Why human security," *Whitehead J. Dipl. & Int'l Rel.* 7 (2006): p. 37.
55. United Nations, *Human Security in Theory and Practice: An Overview of the Human Security Concept and the United Nations Trust Fund for Human Security.*

CHAPTER 2

Countering Transnational Organized Crime

A major security threat has been and will continue to be TOC. The key element is the transnational nature of such illicit operations. In other words, the concern is not only local gangs or drug dealers but also criminal organizations that operate in a transnational nature. According to the National Institute of Justice (NIJ),[1] TOC involves the planning and participation in illicit business endeavors, networks of individuals, or groups who carry out such activities in more than one country.[2] These criminal groups employ the use of systematic violence in order to accomplish their objectives. The crimes committed by TOCs include human smuggling, cybercrime, money laundering, and the trafficking of a range of things: humans, weapons, drugs, endangered species, nuclear materials, and body parts.[3] This chapter examines TOC and the general trends and focuses on how to counter such illicit activities.

Many groups participate in organized crime from guerrilla groups to drug traffickers. Debates have emerged about whether drug trafficking organizations, such as the drug cartels in Mexico or gangs in El Salvador, should be classified as terrorist organizations or narco-terrorists in the case of drug trafficking organizations. It is important to note that terrorism is defined as a tactic with the goal of instilling fear in people. Terrorists generally have political goals. Al Qaeda, for example, seeks to destroy Western civilization.[4] On the other hand, drug traffickers have one goal: to earn money. While the goals of drug traffickers and terrorist organizations are different, there are potential linkages between these organizations. During a March 13, 2002, joint Senate testimony, the assistant secretary

© The Author(s) 2017   17
B. Fonseca, J.D. Rosen, *The New US Security Agenda*,
DOI 10.1007/978-3-319-50194-9_2

for International Narcotics and Law Enforcement Affairs, Rand Beers, and Ambassador-At-Large for Counterterrorism, Francis X. Taylor, explained the symbiotic relationship between organized crime and terrorism, arguing: "There often is a nexus between organized crime and, terrorism including drug trafficking. Links between terrorist organizations and drug traffickers take many forms, ranging from facilitation—protection, transportation, and taxation—to direct trafficking by the terrorist organization itself in order to finance its activities. Traffickers and terrorists have similar logistical needs in terms of material and the covert movement of goods, people and money." They explained how both terrorists and drug traffickers benefit from this relationship, arguing that "[r]elationships between drug traffickers and terrorists benefit both. Drug traffickers benefit from the terrorists' military skills, weapons supply, and access to clandestine organizations. Terrorists gain a source of revenue and expertise in illicit transfer and laundering of proceeds from illicit transactions. Both groups bring corrupt officials whose services provide mutual benefits, such as greater access to fraudulent documents, including passports and customs papers."[5] In sum, there are differences between the goals of terrorist organizations and TOCs but some linkages exist that present major challenges for national security.

Another key difference between organized crime groups and terrorist organizations is the relationship that these groups have with the state. In order to make money, drug trafficking organizations cannot destroy the state because they need the state to survive.[6] Organized crime groups participate in a litany of corrupt activities such as bribing and extorting judges, politicians, and law enforcement officials in order to accomplish their goals. The age-old problem of *plata* or *plomo* (silver or lead) continues: a police officer, judge, or politician can accept a bribe, the *plata*, or they can refuse to participate in corruption and be killed by organized crime groups— hence the *plomo*. The key point here is that organized crime groups have a relationship with the state and need the state. Such organizations thrive in countries where the state apparatus is weak: states plagued with fragile institutions and high levels of impunity and corruption. Criminal groups have a more difficult time functioning when state institutions are robust and institutions work effectively as it becomes harder for these groups to operate by penetrating the state and corrupting government officials, which leads to the corrosion of the state. Experts argue that the nature of the state determines the type of organize crime that operate within the country. Bruce Bagley, a professor at the University of Miami and drug trafficking expert, asserts that "[s]tates determine the form or type of organized crime that can operate and flourish within a given national territory. Criminal organizations, in contrast, do not determine the type of state, although they certainly can deter or inhibit political reform efforts at all levels of a political system."[7] Weak—often young—democracies have a harder time combating organized crime groups as a result of the institutional deficiencies of the state. Bagley emphasizes this point, stating:

> Democratic theorists have only recently begun to seriously examine the problems for democratic transitions that emanate from organized and entrenched criminal networks. In the countries of Latin America and the Caribbean, such neglect of institutional reform may well imperil both political stability and democracy itself. Rather than democratic consolidation, the consequence of ignoring organized crime and its corrosive effects may well be institutional decay or democratic de-institutionalization.[8]

Experts, analysts, and government officials have also analyzed the corrosive capacity of organized crime on democracy itself. Former Mexican President Felipe Calderón (2006–2012) argues "that the expansion and strengthening of transnational organized crime erodes the rule of law and that the damaging consequences of this situation go beyond high crime rates. Organized crime not only deteriorates social order and individual liberties, but it is also a real threat to democracy and the State itself, as it tends to displace and substitute law enforcement agencies and institutions." Calderón emphasizes the fact that organized crime groups can threaten the very survival of the state and negatively impact society due to the high levels of violence. He declares, "At the end of the day, what organized crime does, once it overtakes the government, is extract the rents of society through violence and the threat of it. Once the State has lost control of its own institutions, reality eclipses Hollywood stories of extortion, kidnaping, and killing. The response to this threat must be global through international cooperation mechanisms, and it must definitely involve national and sub national actions."[9] Overall, TOCs seek to earn money and do not desire to destroy Western civilizations like some of the other terrorist organizations, such as ISIS or Al Qaeda. In addition, organized crime groups thrive in areas where the state apparatus is weak and institutions do not function effectively. TOCs need the state and seek to penetrate the state apparatus through various corrupt practices.

THE DARK SIDE OF GLOBALIZATION

While globalization and significant advancements in technology have improved the lives of so many people around the world, there also exists a dark side of globalization. Increased commerce, trade, and more open borders facilitate TOC groups.[10] The NIJ states that "[t]he political turmoil of the 21st century and advances in technology make transnational crime a concern for the United States. Increased travel and trade and advances in telecommunications and computer technology have had the unintended effect of providing avenues for the rapid expansion of transnational organized crime activities. Policing objectives in the United States must extend beyond national borders to seek out and target this type of crime."[11] Take the Internet for example: women and girls can be bought and sold via the World Wide Web. A client, or "John," can search a webpage and explore which person he would like to purchase with the click of a mouse. Many victims are tricked into human trafficking. Judge Herbert B. Dixon Jr. explains how the Internet also can be used to recruit—often through deception—people and trick them into participating in various illicit activities, stating:

> Some trafficking cases start with the offender contacting the potential victims on social networking sites such as Facebook and MySpace. The techniques used by the offenders to gain trust vary widely, including expressing love and admiration of the victim, promising to make the victim a star, and providing a ticket to a new location away from the victim's home. Another type of trafficking effort starts with an online employment search and results in an unsuspecting victim relocating from her home on the promise of an unbelievably good job.[12]

For example, a 19-year-old girl in Illinois seeking to become a model went online and answered an advertisement searching for models. The girl was instructed to wait in a hotel room where it was intended that she would have sexual intercourse with an unknown individual. The perpetrator sought to become this young girl's pimp and sell her in order to profit off this victim. The client was an undercover cop and this teen's nightmare ended, preventing the situation from worsening.[13] This example is one of many that shows how innocent people can become victims as a result of the dark side of the Internet. Therefore, while the Internet facilitates the lives of so many people as communication, business, and travel have become much easier, this resource can be used for criminal activities from human trafficking to terrorism. Dixon Jr. argues that "[t]here have been hopeful signs generated in efforts using the Internet and other technologies to combat human trafficking. However, with each effort to advance the cause of combating human trafficking, the traffickers look for newer technologies to stay a step ahead of law enforcement."[14] Combating such crimes requires law enforcement officials to constantly stay ahead of such activities and abreast of technological changes. Technology is constantly changing and, as a result, there are major challenges.

THE OVER 100-YEAR DRUG WAR

While Richard Nixon officially launched the drug war in 1971,[15] the war on drugs has been an over 100-year war[16] as the Harrison Narcotics Tax Act of 1914 was passed on December 17 of that year. That act involved a tax on all persons who imported, produced, compounded, manufactured, dispensed, distributed, sold, or gave away coca leaves of opium or their derivatives for other purposes.[17] The 1922 Jones-Miller Act outlawed cocaine, but marijuana "became a regulated substance and was ultimately banned through a series of legislative measures from the 1925 Uniform State Narcotics Act and the 1937 Marijuana Tax Act to the introduction of mandatory sentencing laws for the possession of marijuana with the 1952 Boggs Act and the 1956 Narcotics Control Act."[18] Ronald Reagan declared the "modern phase" of the war on drugs in 1982. With the end of the Cold War, the war on drugs became a top national security priority of the US.[19]

THE CASE OF COLOMBIA

Much of the US-led war on drugs has focused on combating coca cultivation, the production of drugs, and drug trafficking in the Andean region. Drugs from Colombia are trafficked to the US. Colombia, which is only a few hours' flight from the US, has been a major security concern for Washington. Colombia is located in a strategic geographic position and insecurity in Colombia could also spill over into other neighboring countries. In addition, Colombia borders the Panama Canal, which is a key commercial shipment zone.[20] Thus, it is important to examine drug trafficking and organized crime in Colombia when talking about US national security and policy with regard to combating organized crime and drug trafficking.

Colombia became an epicenter of organized crime and drug trafficking in the 1990s as a result of the illicit activities of the two major cartels: Medellín and Cali. Pablo Escobar, the ruthless leader of the Medellín cartel, wreaked havoc on the country as he used his wealth, power, and influence to bribe politicians, judges, and police officers to infiltrate nearly every aspect of Colombian society.[21] Escobar and his group of associates murdered presidential candidates and made people offers that they could not refuse: *plata o plomo*; people could accept the bribe and remain alive, or they would be killed—hence the *plomo*. Pablo Escobar was able to penetrate Colombian society so much so that he was an elected official in Congress. Rodrigo Lara Bonilla, the minister of justice, was brave enough to say that Escobar was making a mockery of the Colombian political system, questioning how the Colombian Congress could allow a known drug lord to be a member. Escobar did not take kindly to such remarks and later assassinated this individual. By the early 1990s, Colombia had become one of the most dangerous countries on earth. With the assistance of Washington, the Colombians began an aggressive campaign to topple the major drug cartels by killing the kingpins. This strategy became known as the kingpin strategy and the logic was that law enforcement had to pursue the leaders as the organizations could not function without the kingpins.

The Colombians were able to kill Escobar in 1993 with the support of Washington. The killing of Escobar was viewed as a major victory and eventually led to the downfall of the Medellín cartel. The rival Cali cartel, however, subsequently increased in power but was eventually toppled as well. The collapse of the two major cartels was a "partial victory" at best because Colombia experienced a fragmentation of the criminal organizations: instead of two cartels, Colombia had approximately 300 "cartelitos,"[22] which moved in to fill the void left by the collapse of the two major cartels. In addition, other actors, such as the guerillas in Colombia, particularly the Revolutionary Armed Forces of Colombia (Fuerzas Armadas Revolucionarias de Colombia—FARC), which is the most powerful group, increased their share of the drug trade and control of the industry.

The kingpin strategy is flawed for several reasons.[23] To begin, drug trafficking organizations are nimble and can often adapt to changes in hierarchy. Many people are jockeying for power and seeking to be the next kingpin. Therefore, killing one leader provides other members of the drug cartels with the opportunity to battle for the leadership of the cartel. In turn, the kingpin strategy can lead to more violence because rival cartels can fight amongst each other for control of territory and routes as some may believe that the loss of the leader will create a window of opportunity for other organizations to move in and gain control. In addition, the killing of one capo will not reduce the demand of drugs and undercut the market value. Said differently, drugs will be trafficked as long as demand exists.

The situation in Colombia worsened during the 1990s as drug trafficking and violence increased. Colombia began to experience major economic hardships. By the end of the 1990s, the new Colombian president, Andrés Pastrana (1998–2002), recognized that he needed help and sought international aid in order to end the decades-long internal armed conflict in Colombia and increase security in the country. During this period, Colombia was one of the most dangerous countries in the world and intense debates occurred between experts as to whether or not Colombia was a failed state. Phillip McLean argues that "[i]f failed states on the other side of the globe threaten U.S. interests, then Colombia, a country just two hours by air from Miami, merits priority attention as well. A failed Colombia is truly a scary prospect. Colombia is not a traditional, small, dictator-dominated country, but rather a large, mostly modern nation with a long history of electoral politics and intimate links with the United States."[24] Pastrana sought a Marshall Plan for Colombia, focusing on development, particularly in rural Colombia. The logic was Colombia had to resolve many of its underlying developmental issues. Pastrana asked the Bill Clinton administration for help, and they responded by telling him to write a proposal. President Pastrana's proposal became known as Plan Colombia and was a multi-billion-dollar initiative designed to end the internal armed conflict and decrease levels of violence by increasing security. Drug trafficking was not the major issue for Pastrana as he felt that the internal armed conflict and economic development were the most crucial issues. In other words, the most important thing for Pastrana was to help bring peace to Colombia. Pastrana also believed that you could not isolate the drug problem from the internal armed conflict because the guerrilla organizations were deeply involved in the drug trade. The Clinton administration decided that Plan Colombia would focus on drug trafficking and organized crime as opposed to the internal armed conflict. After delays in the US Congress over human rights concerns, Plan Colombia was passed and signed into law in 2000 by Bill Clinton. However, the final version of Plan Colombia was quite different than the original initiative proposed by Pastrana as 80 percent of the funding went[25] toward what are referred to as "hard" components: equipment and training to the military and other agencies for counternarcotics initiatives as well as aerial spraying campaigns—the spraying of herbicides from airplanes to destroy the cultivation of coca crops, which is the key ingredient in the processing of cocaine.

Plan Colombia evolved over time, particularly with the election of Álvaro Uribe (2002–2010) to the presidency. President Uribe recognized that he had to reformulate the goals of Plan Colombia as the foreign policy of the George W. Bush administration transformed rapidly after the events of September 11, 2001, and the Bush administration's launching of a GWOT.[26] Uribe argued that Colombia did not have an internal armed conflict but instead narco-guerillas or narco-terrorists. Uribe convinced President Bush to become more involved in the Colombian conflict to prevent the situation in Colombia from spiraling out of control. The Colombian president became a crucial ally in the GWOT, which was convenient for the Bush administration because many of the countries in Latin America had taken turns to the left and criticized the Bush administration's foreign policy in the region.

Plan Colombia had triumphs in terms of decreasing homicide rates and increasing levels of insecurity. In 2005, for instance, Colombia had 18,111 national homicides. The number of homicides has continued to decrease over time from 16,140 in 2008 to 13,343 in 2014.[27] In addition, the Uribe administration saw decreases in the number of "terrorist attacks" from 1645 in 2002 to 486 in 2009.[28] The number of kidnappings also decreased from 801 in 2005 to 690 in 2006. Kidnappings continued to decline from 437 in 2008 to 213 in 2009. Kidnappings increased slightly over the previous years but have remained much lower than the 2005 numbers: 282 in 2010 and 288 in 2014.[29] In sum, security in Colombia has increased over time, particularly in terms of homicide levels and kidnappings.[30] However, some experts argue that such security gains are reversible.[31]

EVALUATION OF AERIAL SPRAYING PROGRAMS

The aerial spraying programs have been very controversial as critics have argued that such initiatives have not been effective.[32] Coca cultivation has varied over time, particularly within certain regions in Colombia. Coca cultivation increased from 86,340 hectares in December 2003 to 85,750 in December 2005.[33] In December 2007, Colombia cultivated 98,899 hectares. Coca cultivation dropped in December 2008 to 80,953 hectares. The cultivation of coca continued to decline over time from 73,139 in December 2009 to 48,189 in December 2013.[34] Coca cultivation continued to shift its routes, increasing in some regions and decreasing in others. For instance, in Putumayo, coca cultivation spiked from 7,559 in December 2003 to 12,254 in December 2006. In December 2007, this region recorded 14,813 hectares. Coca cultivation increased from 5,633 hectares in December 2009 to 9,951 hectares in December 2011 in Putumayo. The department of Meta saw cultivation spiked from 12,814 hectares in December 2003 to 18,740 hectares in December 2004, and eventually decreasing to 5,525 hectares in December 2008.[35]

However, coca cultivation increased in other countries in the region. In 2013, Peru surpassed Colombia as the leading cultivator of coca. Natalie Southwick explains the reason for the increasing coca cultivation in Peru, arguing that "[t]he emergence of Peru as the world's main supplier has been boosted by changing consumption patterns. Most Peruvian cocaine is destined for consumption in Brazil and Argentina or export to Europe—all markets that have grown substantially in recent years."[36] However, Colombia overtook Peru as the top coca cultivator in 2015. Coca cultivation spiked to 69,132 hectares in 2014 from 48,000 hectares in 2013, which is an increase of 44 percent.[37]

Drugs continued to be produced and trafficked in Colombia, yet one of the results of the "partial victories"[38] of Plan Colombia was that routes shifted to other countries, such as Mexico. Mexico went up in flames as drug traffickers battled for routes and territory. Thus, while the Uribe administration claimed that Plan Colombia was a model for other countries and other countries can learn lessons from Colombia, the overall drug trafficking situation in the region did not change. Said differently, combating drug trafficking in Colombia has resulted in the routes shifting to other countries.

Colombia's current president, Juan Manuel Santos (2010–2018), has argued that the war on drugs has been a failure in Colombia and called for the need to have a new debate on this issue. Santos has even stated that he is open to legalizing drugs based on scientific research.[39] Santos's rhetoric represents a significant shift from his predecessor, Uribe, who vowed to combat narco-terrorism.

Underlying Challenges in Colombia

Notwithstanding the successes in Colombia, particularly in terms of increasing security and decreasing violence, Colombia still faces various underlying challenges. One of the major obstacles in Colombia has been combating impunity. Despite the fact that Colombia is the oldest democracy in Latin America, the country still faces a litany of obstacles with regard to the implementation of the rule of law as impunity remains high. Experts argue that Colombia has suffered from a culture of impunity for decades. The high levels of impunity have contributed to the vast number of human rights abuses that have occurred in Colombia.[40] The argument is as follows: "Not only are the perpetrators of human rights abuses like massacres and forced displacement not held to account, but those who work to prosecute those perpetrators, including witnesses, lawyers, judges, human rights defenders, families of victims, and prosecutors involved in human rights cases, are regularly threatened and killed."[41] Prosecuting violators of the law, particularly human rights abusers, requires Colombia to strengthen the institutions within the country.

In addition to impunity—and intricately related—is corruption. Colombia continues to have high levels of corruption at all levels of government. According to the Corruption's Perceptions Index, Colombia scored a 37 in 2014 with zero being the most corrupt and 100 being the least corrupt. In terms of the rankings, Colombia ranks 94 out of 175 countries in 2014, with the higher the ranking the higher the level of corruption. In 2012 and 2013, Colombia received a score of 36.[42] Combating corruption requires strengthening institutions. Corruption, therefore, is not simply a cultural issue that is present in various countries, but instead is a major institutional challenge. Said differently, combating corruption and impunity requires strengthening the state apparatus and implementing the rule of law. Corruption levels will decrease when institutions effectively prosecute violators of the law. While strengthening institutions is not a process that happens overnight, it is critical in order for Colombia to combat the high levels of impunity.

DRUG TRAFFICKING AND VIOLENCE IN MEXICO

In addition to Colombia, another country that has been at the epicenter of the US-led war on drugs is Mexico. The issue of drug trafficking and organized crime in Mexico has been a major security issue for many officials in the US as the two countries share a 2,000-mile border.[43] Drugs and violence have spilled over the US-Mexico border, causing concern for US government officials. The topic of drug trafficking and organized crime in Mexico is intricately linked to border security and has been a highly contested issue during the 2016 presidential elections. Donald Trump, the 2016 Republican nominee for president, has emphasized the problem of drugs, organized crime, and illegal immigration at the border and has sought to elevate this issue on the US national security agenda.[44]

Mexico has been engulfed in a drug war, and violence and bloodshed have ensued as drug traffickers battle for control of routes and territory. Drug traffickers are more ruthless and brutal than ever as bodies hanging over bridges with signs warning government officials or rival cartels became a common occurrence. In 2008, a grenade was thrown into a crowd during the Independence Day celebration, demonstrating that nobody is immune from the violence and bloodshed.[45] Drug trafficking and organized crime have spilled over the US border, causing many to be extremely concerned about border security. The US Department of Justice released a report in 2011[46] stating that Mexican drug trafficking organizations operate in over 1,000 cities throughout the US, demonstrating the nature of interdependence between the two countries and showing that drug trafficking and organized crime not only are a problem in Mexico but also impact US security. Experts, however, have argued that such claims are overstated. While Mexican drug trafficking organizations might not operate in 1,000 cities, the organizations still represent a security challenge for law enforcement officials. Scott Higham, Sari Horwitz, and Steven Rich assert that "[t]here is no disputing that Mexican cartels are operating in the United States. Drug policy analysts estimate that about 90 percent of the cocaine, heroin, marijuana and methamphetamine on U.S. streets came here courtesy of the cartels and their distribution networks in Mexico and along the Southwestern border. DEA officials say they have documented numerous cases of cartel activity in Houston, Los Angeles, Chicago and Atlanta."[47] Overall, Mexican drug trafficking organizations represent a security challenge for law enforcement officials.

Drug trafficking is not a new problem in Mexico. In order to understand what unleashed the violence and mayhem, it is important to analyze changes in the political system. From 1929 until 2000, Mexico was controlled by a single party, The Institutional Revolutionary Party (Partido Revolucionario Institucional—PRI). For decades, the PRI dominated all levels of government in Mexico's federal system, which consists of local, state, and federal governments. The PRI was able to keep violence under control by having strong ties with organized criminal groups and negotiating with them. In 2000, Mexico's political system changed drastically as the country transitioned to a democracy with the election of Vicente Fox Quesada of The National Action Party (Partido Acción Nacional—PAN).[48]

While the election of a new party and the transition to democracy appeared to be a step in the right direction, Mexico was plagued by extremely weak institutions from prior to the transition which were ripe with inefficacy, corruption, and lack of transparency. The transition in Mexico can best be described as a flawed transition as corruption has increased as Mexico has become more democratic. While Mexico is a democracy, it is a rather weak democracy with fragile institutions that do not function efficiently.[49]

A problem with counternarcotics strategies, particularly under the Calderón administration, is that such policies have not addressed one of the most pervasive problems in Mexico: corruption. Corruption is commonplace in the country as it exists in nearly all levels of society. Mexico has not managed to decrease its levels of corruption, and, in fact, corruption has increased the more democratic the country has become.[50] In 2014, for instance, Mexico received a score of 34 with 0 being the most corrupt and 100 being very clean. In 2014, Mexico was ranked 103 out of 175 countries according to Transparency International's Corruption Perceptions Index. In 2012 and 2013, Mexico received a score of 34, demonstrating that corruption has continued to be a pervasive problem in the country.[51] Shannon K. O'Neil of the Council on Foreign Relations argues that "[t]he alternation of power at all governmental levels has also helped expose corruption. In the past, new (always PRI) officials would cover for their predecessors and expect those coming after to do the same. But with fierce electoral competition, incoming governments, especially those from opposing political parties, have a strong incentive to publicize the misdeeds (and particularly the overspending) of previous administrations."[52] Despite the alterations in power, corruption remains rampant throughout the country. The problem is that Mexican institutions are extremely weak and do not function effectively. Impunity rates remain very high, demonstrating that Mexicans are not prosecuted for violating the law. Laura Carlsen, the director of the Americas Program at the Center for International Policy, asserts that "[i]n Mexico, 98.3 percent of crimes go unpunished. The justice system has gotten worse, not better, since attempts at reform."[53] The result is that crimes go unpunished and people do not trust the government as a result of learning about countless scandals and acts of corruption. A 2010 survey found that 61.7 percent of Mexicans have little confidence in judges. Only 24.6 percent of Mexicans had high levels of confidence in the Federal Police, while 61.0 had little confidence. The municipal police had the lowest scores with 67.4 percent of the population having little confidence in the institution. The Army and the Navy had the highest levels of confidence in 2010, with 52.5 and 55 percent of the population having high levels of confidence in these institutions, respectively.[54]

The situation in Mexico worsened dramatically when President Calderón launched a war on drugs in order to combat drug trafficking organizations. Calderón had little confidence in the police forces as a result of their inefficiency, high levels of corruption, and lack of preparation. As a result, he relied on the military to combat drug trafficking and organized crime.[55] President Calderón, however, did not fight the drug war alone as Washington sought to help Mexico decrease violence and insecurity. In 2007, the Bush administration financed a $1.4 billion initiative known as the Mérida Initiative. While differences exist between Plan Colombia and the Mérida Initiative, the overall strategies are similar as they both heavily funded "hard" components such as equipment and training. The US government has allocated almost $2.5 billion to the Mérida Initiative from FY 2009 to FY 2015.[56]

The Calderón administration sought to capture the capos of the major drug trafficking organizations in Mexico. Calderón's all-out war on drugs resulted in some victories as 16 kingpins were arrested and three were killed during the Calderón administration, which is a dramatic increase from the seven kingpins arrested during the Fox administration.[57] Calderón marketed the capture of major capos to the Mexican public to demonstrate that his government was winning the war on drugs and making Mexico safer. The problem with the capturing of the kingpins—as witnessed in Colombia—is that it is a hallow victory as other leaders fight to take control of the drug trafficking organizations. Despite the fact that the Calderón administration captured numerous kingpins, violence increased, primarily as a result of the military campaigns against the drug cartels.

The result of the militarization of the drug war has been controversial as drug traffickers and organized crime groups fought not only with the government but also among themselves for control of territory, routes, and control of markets. The end result was that violence in the country increased dramatically. Ted Galen Carpenter argues:

> President Felipe Calderón's decision in December 2006 to have the military launch a full-scale offensive against drug trafficking organizations, though, is a major reason why violence has spiked. Calderón was not the first Mexican president to employ the military against the drug lords, but previous efforts were limited, isolated affairs. His campaign was a massive, militarized attack

on the trafficking empires. Not surprisingly, the cartels have struck back. Critics charge that Calderón used a baseball bat to strike a hornet's nest, and then seemed unprepared when the hornets swarmed out and attacked.[58]

During the presidency of Felipe Calderón, the number of people who died because of the drug war was 70,000, while another 26,000 disappeared.[59] Places like Ciudad Juárez became proverbial warzones as violence became an everyday occurrence. Ciudad Juárez recorded 1,332 homicides in 2008, 2,230 in 2009, and 2,738 in 2010.[60] In 2009, Culiacan, Sinaloa, recorded 476 organized crime-related deaths and an increase in 2010 to 583. In addition, Acapulco, a popular tourist destination located in the state of Guerrero, saw organized crime-related deaths skyrocket from 370 in 2010 to 963 in 2011, representing a 510 percent increase.[61] On the other hand, Juárez had 850 homicides in the same year—a rate of 58 per 100,000 people. Other municipalities also suffered from very high levels of violence in 2012: Culiacan (471); Torreon (792); Chihuahua (587); and Nuevo Laredo (544).[62]

Mexico is an extremely dangerous place for journalists who report on drug trafficking, organized crime, and violence. The goal of criminal actors is to have the least amount of transparency possible. The job of an investigative journalist is to uncover stories. Drug traffickers do not want the population to know about their relationship with corrupt police forces, judges, and other actors and seek to prevent journalists from shedding light on corruption and drug-related violence by silencing them. The number of media-support workers and journalists who have been killed have increased from 11 in 2006 to 14 in 2010.[63] In 2011, two journalists disappeared, while 11 were murdered, 13 were held in illegal detentions, and 17 suffered from forced displacement.[64] According to the Committee to Protect Journalists' 2014 Global Impunity Index, Mexico was ranked as the seventh most dangerous country to be a journalist. The report states that "[j]ustice continued to evade Mexican journalists who face unrelenting violence for reporting on crime and corruption. Sixteen journalists were murdered with complete impunity during the decade and another in 2014. The only relief came last April with the approval of legislation that implements a constitutional amendment giving federal authorities in Mexico broader jurisdiction to prosecute crimes against journalists."[65]

In addition to journalists, Mexican politicians have been murdered for various reasons, from crossing the cartels to speaking out against them. Politicians often find it easier to accept bribes as opposed to working